Faith Hines has a unique insight into the vagaries of gardening life and her sharp wit takes no prisoners. After all: behind every successful gardener is an astonished woman. There is enough wry observation and entertainment here for any gardener ready to throw in the *trowel*.
Crisply turned, each one-liner in this collection is a gem. Full of penetration and wit, this hilarious book will keep you amused ... enough to dig the garden!
A play for Radio 4 has been adapted from *Mrs Murphy's Laws of Gardening*.

Faith Hines is a social historian, archivist, broadcaster and scriptwriter. She also collects laundry machinery. For a period of seven years she was the world's highest paid TV and film model featuring in many well-known advertisements.
She lives with her husband at the Laundry and Mangle Museum, Tunbridge Wells.

By the same author:
Ms Murphy's Law

Mrs Murphy's Laws of Gardening

Faith Hines

*Cartoons by
Gray Jolliffe*

Foreword by
Bob Collard

Temple House Books
Sussex, England

Temple House Books
is an imprint of
The Book Guild Ltd.

Except in one or two instances no effort has been made to determine what may be considered the origin of the material in this book and no responsibility for any such origin is, or can be, assumed.

This book is sold subject to the condition that it shall not, by way of trade or otherwise, be lent, re-sold, hired out, photocopied or held in any retrieval system or otherwise circulated without the publisher's prior consent in any form of binding or cover other than that in which this is published and without a similar condition including this condition being imposed on the subsequent purchaser.

Temple House Books
25 High Street,
Lewes, Sussex

First published 1992
© Faith Hines 1992
Set in Century Schoolbook
Typesetting by Wordset
Hassocks, Sussex

Printed in Great Britain by
Hartnolls Ltd.
Cornwall

A catalogue record for this book is
available from the British Library

ISBN 0 86332 754 0

Contents

Foreword		7
Introduction	How it all began	9
Chapter 1	First Principles	17
2	Going Down in Spades	29
3	Rye Expressions	32
4	The Printed Word	42
5	Holy Weedlock	45
6	Feeding Thoughts	49
7	Liquidity	52
8	Weather or Not	56
9	Pets and Progeny	61
10	Weedology	68
11	Blooming Truths	74
12	Bugs and Blights	79
13	Undercover Revelations	86
14	Produce Principles	91
15	Machination Ruminations	96
16	Trees and Shrubbery	104
17	Garden Decor	109
18	Pot Hunting	116

Acknowledgement

The author thanks Methuen, London,
for permission to use the excerpts
on pages 20 and 96 from
Murphy's Law by Arthur Bloch.

Foreword

Too many people buy the wrong plants, or the wrong seeds, or the right plants and seeds but plant them in the right place at the wrong time or, worse still, in the wrong place at the right time and then S.O.S. Collard's Clinic on BBC Radio Kent asking, for example, how to transplant a thirty-foot tree which is about to demolish their house, or has decided to come indoors for Christmas.

Gardening centres love this type of compulsive gardener, welcoming them back year after year to spend more money on unsuitable trees, shrubs and plants they have to either dig up or lose, simply because they just don't think or plan ahead.

Then there's that army of stalwart ladies who prick out their seedlings in the cold and carefully water them in (some even use warm water, I'm told). How would they like to sit outside in the frost with their tootsies in ice cold water and then, when it freezes, have their pinkies frozen off? I could go on and on!

I'm a gardener of the old school. I learned my trade the hard way – in a walled garden to boot, back in the thirties.

I've said this many times, and will say it again. In fact I call it 'Collard's Law of the Garden' – Gardening is common sense! Bob's Second Law? Keep a sense of humour.

You can live to be a hundred and still not know half of what there is to know about the garden. Even if you're one of those know-it-all Old Adams out there, there's no escaping hard work. Neither will you escape Mrs Murphy's Law – as any gardener severely handicapped with only one set of arms and legs will tell you. Be kind to him or her. Remember, everyone of us is fighting a losing battle.

Bob Collard

Introduction

How it all Began

It was one of those perfect days that occur only in retrospect: the evenings were drawing in and the longest day long gone. A few more weeks and Mrs Murphy's, 'Mend the mower!', 'Isn't it time you fed the roses?', 'Haven't you weeded the plot, yet?' and suchlike would cease. Life could once again return to normal.

Ed pictured winter: drinking his Guinness in front of a blazing fire (for which Mrs Murphy cut excellent apple logs) toasting his toes and relishing the winter TV schedules.

But today was a day for loafing in a chair beneath the leafy apple trees, a drink to hand and a copy of *Gardener's World* at one's side: a day to contemplate the cosmos. Everything, but everything, in the garden was rosy.

Murphy was engaged in these portentous activities when The Voice scored a direct hit.

'Anyone would think you'd been born in a jungle! No wonder we never get apples if you never prune the trees!'

Ed's vision of the cosmos gave a sudden lurch sideways, leaving him with Murphy's First Law of the Garden: Whenever you set out to do anything worthwhile in the garden, something else needs doing first.

Pleased with this new law, he picked up *Gardener's World* (to show his wife that he was doing something).

Meanwhile, Mrs Murphy bustled about, exuding a palpable air of martyrdom. She cut back rampant rock plants, disbudded the chrysanthemums, planted out the winter greens, ridged the leeks and celery, cut out the old wood from the currants, disposed of the wasp-infested windfalls and began effecting temporary repairs to the ornamental arch she had fabricated the year before (with Ed pointing out categorically that, had she used *nails* and not *screws*, she wouldn't have the job to do *now*).

Mrs Murphy asked Ed, **if** he had a moment, to buy some wood preservative. He said he'd get round to it when he'd caught up with *In Your Garden*. But, as it wasn't yet 11 o'clock and the programme didn't begin till four, he wondered whether there was any chance of a cup of coffee?

Mrs Murphy fetched the coffee and, while Ed settled down to enjoy it, she scrubbed the algae off the gnome's wotsit (it was always worst there), removed one supermarket trolley, assorted chewing-gum wrappers, half a shrew and a sodden tennis ball from the pond (dug to Ed's specs. – three feet deep, nine-inch shelves, one part cement, two parts sand, three parts aggregate – he didn't like the look of liners). This pond was all part of Ed's recent drive to save the Greater Crested Newt (someone had casually mentioned that they were changing hands at £50 a time).

By the time Mrs Murphy had cleared the Inconsistent Bladderwort out of the bog garden, she was ready for *her* morning cup of coffee, but decided against it in favour of re-erecting the ornamental screen – flattened by last year's gales (she couldn't stand walking over it once more) – before she finally raked the gravel back on to the paths. She asked Ed to help so that she could get on with the lunch, and Ed decided, quite suddenly, to have a word with Paddy about the mower. Mrs Murphy couldn't argue about that! He promised he would pop down to the village at the same time to pick up a tin of creosote (so as not to hold up his wife that very afternoon).

'What we gardeners expect is climate but what we gets is weather,' warned Ed. Mrs Murphy couldn't argue with that either and agreed the creosoting should be got underway as soon as she could manage it. She asked him to bring back a couple of packs of weed-killer and a couple of pounds of dwarf grass seed, while he was about it, and fixed him another quick coffee (Ed perspired a lot and found it tedious work, sunbathing in late August). Then she set about putting away the conglomeration of saws, hammers, chisels, screwdrivers and nails (she couldn't imagine what the mallet was for) which the little Murphys had spirited out of the shed to bury the deceased and dewinged gossamer moth in a suitably inscribed matchbox (the usual full-blown service – flowers, lettered cross, etc.). Then she replanted the catmint the new kittens had discovered for the third time that week and, on her way to the kitchen, lifted a couple of rows of spuds for lunch, and finally escaped indoors to 'relax' over a little housework (Ed could never understand what she could find to do).

Mr Murphy, without creosote, lawn seed or weed-killer, came in just as the table had been laid and the food was ready to serve. He said he wasn't very hungry; in any case, it was the same as he had had just two minutes ago down at The Bull (he couldn't afford to offend Paddy, now could he?). All the same, the walk had left him a little peckish and, as it was too late to do anything with the mower (without ruining the meal), and to keep Mrs Murphy happy (so he said), he sat down, finished his and was ready to leave the table before Mrs Murphy had dished hers.

Not wanting to be 'in the way', as Ed put it, while she coped with flying mash from the youngest, and separated Heinz baked beans from the streaming nose of the eldest, Ed called for a Guinness in the garden and retired to his favourite place, the orchard, under the apple trees, to rest midst nature's mellow beneficence and to digest (so he said) *Gardener's Weekly*.

'Don't forget the mower!' Mrs Murphy bawled after him. 'And those hollyhocks need staking!'

'Silly flowers are only tended by blooming idiots,' muttered Murphy under his breath, as he thankfully lowered himself into the depths of the only deck-chair, obscured from the house by thistles, wild flowers, herbs and grasses that, without competition from cultivated varieties, grew far more impressively than in the wild – so much so that it was virtually impossible to distinguish the wild from the cultivated. 'Thistle do!' chuckled Mr Murphy, a witty man.

By the time his wife had surfaced (carrying Ed's second Guinness of the afternoon), the interim periods filled with her banging on about 'Adam didn't create Eve for gardening', the IDEA had struck.

Tearing himself from page three, cunningly positioned as the centrefold of the 'Apples' supplement, Ed pulled Mrs Murphy on to his knee. 'Of course the Lord didn't create women just for *gardening*!' She thought he was being filthy and jumped up quickly.

'Our little acre – God's little acre,' Ed corrected himself, 'has been entrusted to us for the cultivation of cowslips, primroses, bluebells, cuckoo-flowers and all those wild plants you love so much. It is the natural home of clovers, violets, saxifrage and wild grasses!'

Slyly refreshing his memory from the article in front of him he continued, 'Wild herbs and flowers, which nowadays uneducated people consider common-or-garden weeds, were once used to make up the traditional English garden. You – and millions like you – may expect to find wild flowers in wild places. Not me!

'As an official Protector of newts, toads and frogs, I am pleased to see weeds in orderly beds of cultivated flowers. Saving our wild plants and our grasses for our children will preserve the moths, butterflies and wildlife in general which rely on them for their children's children.'

Mrs Murphy had never heard Ed utter so much rubbish in one breath. Her mind shot back to the lifeless gossamer moth Ed had that morning swotted and flattened with the Fauna and Flora Preservation Society's brochure. All male Murphys shrank at the merest reference to 'creepy-crawlies', and the only reason they'd never holidayed abroad was because they hated anything with wings. Ed wasn't that fond of water either. She smelt a very large rat.

'Wild flowers belongs in wild places, not in cultivated

gardens. Especially not ours. Blooming dandelions, nettles and daisies are the enemy of the gardener!'

Mrs M. might just as well have saved her breath. Her attempts to rid the orchard and garden of the invading jungle of noxious weeds were truly thwarted when Ed won the support and approval of the Nature Conservancy Council. Photographers visited to record the event – mass media literally covered the garden.

The shift in agricultural patterns had, to all intents and purposes, heralded the disappearance of thousands upon thousands of acres of woodland and meadows to reappear on one-third of an acre – the Murphy plot.

Ed, greatly impressed by some singer, was busy contemplating a 'Weed-Aid' sit-in for Africa. TV interviews were fixed. Talks were in progress for a new programme for Channel 4 – *Thistle Do*. Things were beginning to get out of hand.

When Mrs M. dropped her stand against multilateral weed emancipation ('Bring back the dandelion!', 'Why waste valuable land cultivating vegetables when wild ones grow free?') and set to with a will – planting nettles, propagating chickweed, sowing wild parsnips, pricking out hogweed and generally encouraging the proliferation of hundreds of wild herbs, vegetables and spices – Ed sensed danger with a capital F for work.

The leisured puffing of the Dublin-Limerick Express, the drowse of the bee-glade, were fast becoming a pipe dream.

Soon the Murphy cupboards boasted a veritable hoard of homeopathic remedies, tisanes, powders, snore cures and poultices. Braised dandelion roots accompanied the Sunday (lentil) roast. After all, dandelions provide more vitamin C than any other fruit or vegetable AND, Mrs Murphy was at no pains to point out, *every part* can be eaten . . . and didn't the vet say Ed was short on vitamin C? No salad was complete without the basic nettle and chickweed.

Fat-hen, comfrey and hi-weed replaced spinach as a 'good green veg.' (come to that, Ed hated spinach, too).

'If it's bitter, it must be good for you,' stressed his wife. (Ed lacked iron.)

The day that the knapweed tisane, lovingly prepared by Mrs Murphy to cure her husband's hangover, frightened Ed better (it was also the day that the national press covered 'The Long and Successful Tradition of British Folk Medicine', using the Murphys' lead as an example), Ed's wild garden, now flourishing in colourful, random abandon, was scheduled for extermination.

Talk of exporting weeds to needy countries was forgotten. Ed's previous year's Christmas present to his wife (a long-handled scythe) mysteriously appeared.

Paddy was asked to mend the lawnmower.

First for the chop was the crop that had replaced the hops (Mrs Murphy had read that it made an excellent substitute for beer-making), followed closely by herbs for tea and coffee, the tubers to make your hair grow and the Sunday weed-roast: leaves to make you see in the dark and the stalks that kept Ed 'regular'.

Now that they are on speaking terms again (Mrs Murphy didn't have the heart or the inclination to make Ed scythe down the tall grass, thistles and nettles around his tree in the orchard), life is back to normal. It's another of those perfect days that occur only in retrospect: the afternoon sun unobstructed by cloud, a soft and scented breeze – distance lending enchantment to the even purr of the Qualcast Suffolk Punch, the absence of children. It's a day for sprawling in a chair, beneath unpruned trees, a glass of Guinness to hand and the *Irish Times* abandoned on the uncut grass: a day to look upon the cosmos and relish the fact that everything in the garden is rosy.

Murphy is doing just that when The Voice hits. 'When are you going to pick the apples? Fruit pies don't come wrapped in rough-puff pastry, you know!'

Under his breath, Ed mutters his wife's favourite gardening law: 'There's never enough time to do anything in the garden properly. If anything can go wrong in the garden – it will!'

In the background, scything away the nettles, The Voice adds, '. . . and when it does, it won't be this woman who puts it right!' and she sweetly hands the scythe to Ed, blade first.

The Murphys have gleaned important lessons that they feel the world's gardeners could benefit from, and laws of the garden which amateur gardeners have been waiting to see formally expressed (in printable language) for years.

Here, then, is a selection of the truths which the Murphys discovered – the back-breaking way.

Faith Hines

Backache can be heard but not seen

1

First Principles

MURPHY'S BASIC GARDENING LAW
Whenever you set out to do anything worthwhile in the garden, something else needs doing first.

Corollaries
1. There is never enough time to do it right.
2. It's too late to do it again.
3. If there's enough time and you're not too late, it will rain.

MRS MURPHY'S BASIC GARDENING LAW
If anything can go wrong in the garden, it will.

Corollary
Every solution breeds new blight.

BACK BASICS
Backache is invisible.

Corollaries
1. Backache can be heard but not seen.
2. The one certain thing about backache is gardening.

IMMORTALITY RULES
1. Old gardeners never die – they just smell away.
2. Biennials have a two-year life cycle: you sow the seed in the spring for flowers the following year. The plants then form seed pods and die. Any fool knows it is impossible to get rid of biennials.

FAITH'S FIRST GARDENING LAW
You can cultivate the plot until your fingers turn green: if you can get it to weed itself, patent the method quick.

Corollary
If you can get the lawn to mow itself then you've got a sure-fire winner.

FALL-BACK POSITION
You *can* grow anything.

Corollary
Nothing is easier.

MRS FORSTER'S MULLED WHINE
Procrastination in the garden is psychiatric couch grass.

MRS BROWN'S BASIC LAWS OF GARDENING
1. Never plant anything in the garden that can subsequently be held against you.
2. Birds can be fooled once . . . the family pet, *never*.
3. A man who helps with the weeding is up to something.
4. Men who have difficulty making a start in the garden have no trouble at all with the motorbike or car.
5. No matter who plants it, you'll end up peeling it.

6. 'Popping down the road to borrow Fred's tools.' translated means, 'Popping down to the pub, and should I by chance see Fred I'll ask if I can borrow his tools.'

Corollary
Fred is always in the pub.

Always plead ignorance

MEN'S PROBLEMS
Anything in the garden is either blistering, crippling or gives you backache.

Corollary
Most men develop backache, crippling cramps and blisters from the moment they leave the office on Friday until they greet their secretaries on Monday at nine. Any pain will strike precisely where it will be aggravated by every suggested gardening chore. It won't affect sex.

SOD'S LAW
Profanity is the language the gardener knows best.

THE RELUCTANT GARDENER'S MAXIMS
1. Never weed or mow unnecessarily . . . it stimulates growth.
2. Never put off until tomorrow what you can avoid altogether.
3. If your wife demonstrates how it should be done . . . praise how much better she does it and let her.
4. Always plead ignorance.
5. When in doubt, switch on the TV.
6. There's always the pub.

ED MURPHY'S SABBATH LAW
I weed the beds, mow the lawn, water the borders, trim the hedges almost every day.
Almost Monday.
Almost Tuesday.
Almost Wednesday.
Almost Thursday.
Almost Friday.
Almost Saturday.
Sunday is a day of rest.

EHRMAN'S COMMENTARY
1. Things will get worse before they get better.
2. What makes you think things will ever get better? (From *Murphy's Law* by Arthur Bloch).

FAITH'S EXPERIMENTAL TRUTHS
1. Horticultural experiments should be reproducible – they should fail consistently in the same way.
2. If by any chance any experiment works for the amateur gardener, any good gardening book will tell

him or her exactly where they went wrong.

THE PHILOSOPHY OF GREENS

1. The keen gardener knows that God probably had the consideration that green vegetables lack protein in mind when he invented matching caterpillars.

2. Sally on spinach: If God had intended mummy to make us eat dandelions and spinach he'd have planted them in the Garden of Eden.

3. Colin on brassica: The size of mum's spring greens bears no relationship to the amount of bubble and squeak she turns out every Monday.

4. A vampire's view: We are poor, unfortunate, unloved mammals suffering from iron deficiency because the bleeding kids eat the spinach. The ideal date is one that turns into lasagne verde at midnight.

GUEST'S LAW
The visitor to the garden is assured of two things:
1. The best are over.
2. The good ones have gone.

LAW OF THE REAL ESTATE
Perfection in a garden is achieved by the gardener about to sell his property.

THOUGHTS FROM A HAMMOCK
1. Life is what passes you by when you are gardening.
2. Gardening by choice is like an open prison from which you wish you could escape.

PLOT SABOTAGE
Leave an immaculately tended garden alone for a long weekend and before you've reached the end of the road it will have outgrown its stakes, done a deal with the Weedex, advertised 'Cafe Open' to all rootpests, cutworms, millipedes, wireworms, weevil grubs, slugs and carrotfly, and moss and clover will have overgrown lawns and paths if the algae don't get there first.

MRS BROWN'S GARDENING DICTUM
Any gardener with only two arms and two legs is severely handicapped.

BEFRIENDING PRINCIPLE
When an army of slugs wipes out the lettuce patch, address each by name. It is better to be regarded as a conservationist than a gardener.

SUE'S PSYCHIC DISCOVERY
The only sure way to have the plants you want in the garden is to tell the weeds that they're prize specimens and the plants you prize that they're weeds.

A RUSTIC RUMINANT
Be kind to the gardener – remember, every one you meet is fighting a losing battle.

Corollary
Even a bad gardener will achieve success once in a while. He or she will not recognize it – neither will anyone else, if they're cute.

ROBIN'S LAST LAUGH
Since the early bird catches the worm, you'd think the stupid worm would have a lie-in.

WEEKEND PLATITUDES
1. Come day, go day, God send Monday.
2. Two-sevenths of our life is spent at the weekend.

BIRTH OF THE BLUES
True gardening is like labour: sheer hard work, but without the aid of gas and air.

MARY'S CONTRARY LAW
Vegetable plots grow until they exceed the capability of the person who must maintain them.

BARGAIN ABASEMENTS
1. Avoid any nursery advertising 'While Stocks Last'.
2. 'Bargain of the Week': something you cannot possibly use at a price you cannot possibly refuse.

Squire's law

KNOWALL'S LAW
The gardener who thinks he knows it all is especially annoying to us folk who really do.

LUMBER'S BELL LAW
Door bells and telephones are contrivances invented to irritate the keen gardener. A bell will ring only when you are:

1. Knee-deep in clay or dung.

2. In the middle of a bud graft.
3. Just about to label the seeds you've sown.

Whatever the reason, the call won't be for you. The knock on the door is to deliver your neighbour's registered parcel.

LABORIOUS CONCLUSION
The haves and the have-nots in the garden can be traced back to the dids and the did-nots.

SQUIRE'S LAW
People who least need allotments have allotments.
People who can least afford a large garden have large gardens.
People who have small gardens can afford a gardener.

WOT'S COOKING LAW
Women gardeners are like pressure cookers: you ain't seen nuffin' until they blow their top.

LAW OF THE UNIVERSE
Other planets may not be able to support life, but then it's not that easy in our garden either.

LAW OF THE OPTIMIST
Good must ultimately prevail over evil. This is the belief of all novice gardeners.

Corollaries
1. Past experiences rarely make for future confidences in the garden.
2. Experience enables you to recognize a mistake when you make it again.

REGULAR'S LAW
The number of times you 'gotta go' has a direct correlation with the rhubarb and onion seasons (from *1,001 Logical Laws*, Logical Machine Corporation, 1978, Doubleday and Company, Inc.)

Corollary
Rhubarb reaches the parts that Heineken daren't mention.

LAW OF THE STATELY HOME
When a visitor to the garden of a stately edifice trips and damages a limb, he or she worries about the injury. The gardener worries about the plant.

USEFUL LAWS OF GARDEN GAMBLING
1. If anything dies it's a stroke of bad luck.
2. If anything grows it's a fluke.

LAW OF THE OVERGROWN PATCH
Always know where the gate is.

BASIC LAW OF HORTICULTURE
It has been established beyond any reasonable doubt that everything grows better if it's been planted – that's if it grows at all.

Corollaries
1. Amateur gardeners plant anything that will grow well, regardless of the family's tastes. Serious gardeners prefer to keep the garden well-stocked and don't plant anything which runs the slightest risk of being picked, cooked and eaten.
2. Every gardener grows something he doesn't like just because it's foolproof.
3. If, in the course of the British growing season, the

family gardener actually produces something that all the family really enjoys, e.g. melons, only three will grow large enough and sweet enough to eat; all three will mature on the same day.

LAW OF EQUILIBRIUM
Time is nature's way of keeping everything from happening at once. Tell that to the guy who invented the basic law of horticulture!

SEED BED TRUISM
Any small, solid object in a well-prepared, finely-raked tilth migrates to sit directly on top of ungerminated seed. If the seeds are sown one every four inches in a meticulously drawn drill, the solid objects will be similarly dispersed in a dead straight line.

Corollary
Seed germination can be likened to a pair of socks – you need at least three of the same kind to make sure of having two.

GARDENER'S DILEMMA
Where gardening is concerned, no matter what you do, how much you do, or how you do it, it is never enough.

Corollaries
1. What you haven't done is always more important than what you have done.
2. Smile – if they had germinated, most of them would be dead by now anyway.
3. If you don't eat them something else will.

PHILOSOPHER'S CONCLUSION
A gardener is an idealist who never quite makes it.

NEW GARDENER'S DILEMMA
One only realizes the nasturtiums are marigolds when they bloom. This eventually brings out the basic dishonesty in gardeners.

LAW OF PRINCES
Gardening has been the delight of kings and philosophers. Gardening is the chosen activity of snobs and drudges.

Gardener's dilemma

2

Going Down in Spades

TOUGH THOUGHTS
An erection is like digging the garden; the more you think about it, the harder it gets.

THE UNSEEN DANGER
Backache is invisible.

Corollary
If you really want to get out of digging the garden, you'll have to chop off your toes before she'll believe you're physically unfit.

LAW OF LUMBAR
In spite of what the experts write, digging is downhill all the way. The more and the better you dig, the more work you create.

Corollary
Digging, like housework, is self-destructive.

FIRST RULE OF DON'T LET THE DAISIES GROW UNDER YOUR FEET
A short cut in digging is the shortest cut between digging and hoeing.

AU GRAND SOLEIL

The only thing ever accomplished in the undug garden is getting browned off on sunny, unmown lawns. The greatest accomplishments stem from those who can afford to pay others to do it. The nicest thing about watching others work in the garden is that it gives you something to do.

Au Grand Soleil

DIGGING FOR VICTORY LAWS
1. If it's worth digging for it's worth killing for.
2. If it's worth fighting for it's worth fighting dirty for.

TILL'S LAW
　It's easier to cultivate a garden than to dig it.

　Corollary
　Digging takes longer than you think. So does peeling the spuds he grows.

THE INTELLIGENT CAT FALLACY
　Cats have this strange idea that a newly dug, raked and sown patch of earth is a feline latrine.

THOUGHT IN FRONT OF A BLAZING LOG FIRE ON A WINTER'S NIGHT
　A long, fine weekend is just what is needed to make a start on the digging.

SECOND THOUGHT
　Keep on snowing.

3

Rye Expressions

BESOM'S TRUISM
No matter how much dust you sweep under the carpet, you still can't sweep leaves under the lawn.

THE LAW OF BETTER LATE THAN NEVER
To estimate the time it takes to get the grass cut it is first necessary to estimate the time you think it should take – for example an hour. Next, swap the unit of measurement (in this case hours) with the next highest unit (in this case days). It follows, therefore, that in order to get the grass cut on a given Sunday, nagging should commence the preceding Friday.

Corollaries
1. Progress is made on alternate Fridays.
2. The amount of lawn one man can mow in one morning is in direct proportion to opening hours, breed of dog and the fishing, hunting and shooting season.

THE PRO-AM LAW
The fundamental difference between the professional and the amateur is that the professional knows just where, and how hard, to kick the mower – whereas the amateur

The pro-am law

knows to let well alone.

Corollary
The mowing of any lawn varies inversely with the fundamental ability of the mower to take an interest.

GRASS WIDOW DEFINITION
A wife temporarily parted from her spouse while she mows the lawn and he seeks greener pastures.

DIVORCEE'S COROLLARY TO GRASS WIDOW DEFINITION
The young grass on the other side of the fence, though probably greener, is covered with cow-pats. Men won't notice this fact until they're knee-deep in manure and fungus.

LAW OF TWINNING
Identical mowers bought by you and your neighbour from

the same store at the same time and tested in an identical manner will not behave in an identical fashion: his will work; yours won't.

Corollary
Murphy's Mechanical Law of Gardening now applies – Other people's tools work only in other people's gardens.

ADAM'S CONCLUSION
Rationalization is a mental technique which allows one to lie, cheat or make excuses about not mowing the lawn whilst sitting on it and looking at it, without feeling guilty.

LAW OF THE BLUNT INSTRUMENT
Even the most versatile and expensive of lawnmowers, which leave no stone unturned, will be unable to cope with grass along walls and fences, under hedges, around trees, down ditches and steep banks.

LAWS OF LAWN CLEARANCE
1. Any lawn cleared thoroughly of coarse grass and moss will reveal an area of mud supporting deep-rooted plantains.
2. Mud patches never need mowing.
3. The cleared lawn reveals that there was no cultivated grass in the first place.

GOTCHA LAW
If the electric lawnmower functions perfectly in the garden centre from which it was purchased, it will subsequently malfunction the minute you get it home, e.g. grassbox won't fit/stay on/capacity too small for mower size; lead won't stretch across concrete patio.

Sodding laws (1)

CLAMP AND THREE SCREWS IDIOM
The mower-sharpener designed to easily sharpen any size, shape, age or type of mower will not fit yours.

LAW OF NO RETURN
The difference between a recoil start and an electric start plus 12-volt battery is that dad can start the mower.

Corollaries
1. The question about a motor with first-time starting, better carburettor, replaceable filter and power-lubrication system, is when is somebody ever going to get up off his backside and use it?
2. Little Johnnie thinks the new motor mower is a racing car. The lawn thinks it's Brands Thatch.

MARRIAGE GUIDANCE LAW OF ENERGY CONSERVATION

A major cause of marriage breakdown is a man's inability to get the mower moving on Sunday. An energy crisis can and will produce a manual power cut.

SODDING LAWS

Having decided that your new lawn will be turfed, and having therefore dug, manured and finely raked the site to ensure a weed-free receptive surface for the turfs, you will find that the turfing contractor will either:

1. Deliver the fortnight you told him you would be away in the Sahara on holiday. On your return the turfs look like wizened coconut matting.

2. Deliver six weeks later than promised by which time the carefully prepared site is knee-deep in noxious weeds and needs digging and raking all over again.

3. If you haven't had time to prepare the ground, deliver the turfs two weeks early and in a drought.

4. If none of the above applies, the turfs will be delivered either at the furthest possible distance away from where they are to be laid or at the wrong address.

Whichever of these occurs, it will be your fault and the bill must be paid.

Corollary
The minute the turf is successfully laid, the sprinkler erected and the contractor's instructions not to walk on the new turf for two weeks are about to be faithfully observed, while you are out purchasing the new hose to keep the grass in good condition, your entire family of grandchildren will descend unexpectedly, complete with dogs and bats and balls and a very special picnic to eat on the lawn to save gran cooking.

SEED'S LAW OF SOD IT ALL
When you have painstakingly distributed the lawn seed at the precise rate, lightly raked it in, patted it all down dexterously and lightly with the back of a spade, clipped it back with shears when it has successfully attained two luscious inches and are sitting back patiently waiting to repeat the process twice before the first eagerly anticipated mow, some idiot will shave it close with the mower on the lowest setting, criticizing your ability to mow a lawn properly.

Corollaries
1. A mow in time saves nine and counting to ten.
2. No matter how splendid, how short, how beautifully rolled and manicured the lawn looks now, within minutes it will look as if it hadn't been recently done and, in a matter of hours, will look as if it needs mowing again.

FRED BARE'S LAW OF DESQUAMATION
With a lawn laid from turf, one must expect coarse weeds to a greater or lesser degree, whereas a lawn raised from seed is usually quite free from weeds and, often, quite free from grass.

FAITH'S NOTE
Seed is best covered lightly with a little dry, sifted soil laid by for the purpose and then gently patted in with the back of a spade. The allowance of seed should be one ounce to every square yard. This should be adequate to feed a family of house sparrows for approximately one week.

WIMBLEDON HOPES
If you long for a lawn like those smooth but tough championship courts, you can make no better start than

sowing the same seed as that used by the All England Club. The only small difference will be that football cup finals and trench warfare are played out on yours.

I'm very sorry but we're right out of lawnmower fuel

Saving graces

FAIRWEATHER MAXIMS

If you can get out to mow before it rains either the fuel runs out or the electricity fails. It will not be the fault of the machine or you. This phenomenom can be timed by the cunning.

CUTTING LAWS
1. Electric mowers don't work any better plugged in.
2. Mowers may be made to work if you fiddle long enough with them by which time various rules are waiting to rear their heads:

   a. The Rule of Too Wet to Mow without Damage to the Grass.

   b. The Rule of It's Too Dark to See Now.

   c. The Rule of Don't Wake the Children.

   d. The Rule of Beware! Frog and toad mating season.

SAVING GRACES
When a petrol mower has been fully overhauled and re-assembled and is known to work, the following will apply:
1. The fuel tank will be empty. You've lost the can, so can't go for more fuel.
2. If, in the unlikely circumstance that you have a suitable can, the garage will be closed, or sold out.
3. If, in the most exceptional circumstances, you have a standby electric mower, this is the weekend that the national grid announces its summer recess.

THE LAW OF GRASS ROOTS
No man's life, liberty or sanity are safe while the mowing season is in full swing.

Corollary
An Englishman's home may well be his castle but the right to mow the lawn *alone*, and in *peace*, when *you* want to, is the greatest of all freedoms.

LAWS OF SILENCE
1. It is difficult to ignore the sound of your neighbour mowing his lawn.
2. To make a man feel guilty – make a noise like a mower.

DIGITAL LAW
Flymos like toes.

PETER'S LITTLE-KNOWN FACTS OF THE GREENSWARD
1. Never let a motor mower know you're in a hurry.
2. A promise is a curious thing – it won't work unless you do.
3. Just because the lawn was mowed twice last week proves nothing.
4. Never Flymo through the tulips.
5. Look after the molehills – the anthills will look after themselves.

MATHEMATICAL GROUNDS
1. Twenty per cent of the clergy mow their own lawns; the other eighty per cent pray for it to be done.
2. Eighty per cent of bishops mow their own lawns; the other twenty per cent pay for it.
3. Six out of every ten women mow with a Flymo. What the other four do with it isn't recorded.

PAT'S LAW
A Guernsey cow makes a grand lawn moo-er.

HALF-TIME RULE
Whenever a mower is reminded to complete the mowing, the reminder will come in between innings, halves or sets.

RATE'S TRUISM
The grass may well be greener and shorter on the other side of the fence, but you paid your rates for the privilege of growing yours yellower and longer.

LAW OF THE LEARNER DRIVER
It's not mowing the lawn that bothers me – it's the people I run into.

Corollary
If your wife insists on mowing the lawn – don't be the first to stand in her way.

Law of the learner driver

4

The Printed Word

MRS BROWN'S ALL-ENCOMPASSING LAW OF GARDENING
Gardening is like pregnancy: it is nothing like the book.

MR MURPHY'S LITERARY VIEW
Gardening books should not be set aside lightly: they should be hurled with great force.

THE NOW-YOU-SEE-IT RULE
The only reference materials lost by lending are the specialist notes you wanted to keep. If, by chance, you happen to see the subject serialized in a feature article in a newspaper or magazine, the printer's current strike will ensure that the vital piece you were most anxious to cut out and keep to complete your programme, is in the issue affected. If it isn't, a reduced press-run ensures that your district is the only one not circulated. Should you be able to replace the leaflet, one or more of the following apply:

1. It was located or returned – your wife forgot to say.
2. It's in the same place you couldn't find it last time – where you knew you wouldn't forget it.
3. It's been protecting the seedlings you were raising –

they are now dead from lack of light.

4. The up-to-the-minute version was published that week.

LAW OF THE BOOKWORM

Progress in the garden varies inversely with the number of books, gadgets and gizmos on offer in the *Sunday Express*.

Hi, I'm splongimonius frangiformis abnoxifrons culpidae. Who are you?

FOUR LAWS OF OBFUSCATION

1. There are no real secrets to cultivation – only plots.

2. For counter-instructions read every good Gardening Authority.

3. For subtle distinctions (pinched from every good Gardening Authority) read the Sunday supplements.

4. For contrary advice, listen to 'her indoors's' interpretation of the plagiarism in the Sunday supplements.

MRS MURPHY'S PLEA
Let's campaign for real English in the garden and forget about all this Latin rubbish.

Corollaries
1. If written in English, Latin names are perfectly comprehensible.

2. By the time you've learnt the Latin name, they've changed it.

3. If you do not understand a word in a particular amateur gardening handbook, ignore it: the sentence will make perfect sense without it.

4. The longer and more unpronounceable the name, the more mundane the plant.

5

Holy Weedlock

THE BASIC LAW OF HOLY WEEDLOCK
The best training for gardening is marriage.

Corollaries
1. Behind every successful gardener is an astonished woman.
2. About the only way to get a gardener nowadays is to marry one.
3. Gardening is a process by which a man finds out what sort of husband his wife thinks she ought to have married.

EVERY WIFE'S LAMENT
Gardening expands to exclude all more interesting possibilities.

LAW OF THE UNWELCOME ARRIVAL OF SPRING
There is nothing so harrowing to the soul of the average married man as the first growth of lawn grass.

LAW OF ADULTERY
One green finger too many has ruined many a formal bed.

OLD PROVERB UPDATED

A man's place is in the garden. He should go there as soon as he's finished the washing-up.

Corollaries
1. Most men are saved from washing-up and gardening by being inept at both.
2. The garden is full of willing people . . . some willing to work, the remainder willing to let them.

PANSY'S PONDER

Intuition is that which enables the amateur husband to arrive at the most irrefutable, dogmatic, irrevocable gardening decision without the aid of common sense.

SACROSANCTITY

Before a couple marry, the man gives his sweetheart flowers. Afterwards, she has to buy her own, even

Sacrosanctity

though the garden's full of them: 'I didn't grow those prize blooms for you to go cutting them all off!'

MRS MURPHY'S VIEW ON MARRIAGE
It is easier to effect a repair on the M25 substrata than to get the garden dug.

ED'S REPLY TO MRS MURPHY'S VIEW ON MARRIAGE
It's pleasant to watch someone else digging. It gives you something pleasing to do – a reason for an early bath, for example.

LAW OF SEXES
Depression in women is caused by the menstrual flow. Depression in men also follows a monthly cycle according to what gardening chores are due, e.g.

January – finish digging not started.

February – sow broadbeans and shallots not planted last year.

March – cut back evergreens which have overgrown their stations.

April – dig ground still not yet dug for planting seed potatoes, etc.

MRS WRIGHT'S ERRATUM
In the books, you'd be sitting in the deck-chair surrounded by gracious lawns and embowered with fragrant blossoms. In real life, you're on your hands and knees weeding while your husband reclines in the chair reading the book which shows you sitting in the chair embowered by blossoms.

MRS WISE'S SECOND CAVEAT
Men like the idea of a garden. They just didn't realize it would last so long.

DAFFODIL'S MAINTENANCE TRUISM
A female may not always be able to fix a faulty machine. She will, however, know just where to find the staples, sellotape, superglue, string and sealing-wax she fixes everything else with.

BUDGETARY POSER
The biggest mystery to a gardener's wife is how her husband spends more on feeding the crops than it costs to buy fresh vegetables.

SILLY QUESTION
Wife to husband weeding in torrential rain. 'This is probably another of my stupid questions, but can't you do that indoors?'

BUCK-PASSER'S LAW
The gardener who smiles when things go wrong knows there's a wife he can blame it on.

TIRED TILLER'S MAXIM
A gardener can be said to be tired when s/he empties the weed-killer into the fertilizer bucket.

6

Feeding Thoughts

ADAM'S ADMONITION
Those who enjoy the fruits of labour shouldn't watch the patch being manured.

Corollary
Don't let muck-spreading rub off on you.

FIRST RULE OF FEEDING
Avoid treading in anything soft.

First rule of feeding

NEWTON'S LITTLE-KNOWN SECOND LAW
Whichever way you spread manure it'll be upwind.

Corollary
Spadeful for spadeful, manure is as lethal as gunsmoke.

NFU AXIOM
The public is an insensitive body which mindlessly objects to being poisoned by nitrates, choked to death by burning stubble, deformed by steroids, and paying farmers too much for growing food nobody wants.

MURPHY'S LAW OF RESTRAINED INVOLVEMENT
1. Don't get any on you.
2. Keep a spade's throw away from manure.
3. To keep flies out of the kitchen, keep dung in the sitting room.
4. Dung sounds like a bell but it doesn't have a sweet ring.

DUNG ROMIN'
Some people think manure makes plants grow. It does. The plants are trying to escape the smell.

FEED AND WEED RULES
1. Liquid ounces are measured in litres.
2. Metric packs treat square feet.

ICI'S UNWRITTEN LAW
A fertilizer is a man-made substance that when applied to a given shrub produces a scientific paper.

GARDENER'S SCIENTIFIC MAXIM
If it can't be done with a packet of chemicals it is not worth doing.

LAW OF CHANCE IS A FINE THING
It *is* possible to leave a plant or shrub unwatered and unfed with no effect on its growth or flavour or flowers whatsoever. No gardener will believe you.

ILLEGAL SUBSTANCES
Any synthetic 'special' fertilizer which effectively feeds and fuels everything that grows, is banned by civil servants and politicians.

Corollaries
1. In the unlikely event it is not banned, someone will claim the growth it stimulates is malignant.
2. Within the next decade it will be proved statistically by civil servants and politicians that A.I.D.S. is transferred by application of natural manure.
3. Someone or something will raise a stink.

TAINT'S LAW
The compost bin guaranteed to quickly rot waste will:
1. Rot or disintegrate before the compost is mature.
2. Overflow on the first day of use.
3. Harbour the largest hornets' nest in Christendom.

THE LAW OF MATTER
One hundred per cent organic, super-concentrated, specially composted and guaranteed weed-free manure will nourish your existing weeds to a spectacular size.

THE LAW OF SOLIDS
A barrowful of mephitic manure twenty-five yards square is capable of treating an area twenty-five miles wide.

Corollary
Muck spreading always coincides with the year's windiest day.

7

Liquidity

SQUARE PEG LAW
   Universal tap connectors will fit everybody's tap . . . except yours.

HAZEL TWIG TRUISM
   To err is human.
   To find water divine!

FIRST LAW OF WATERING
   Things get worse under pressure.

   Corollary
   Seeds sown thinly and evenly in a neat, straight line on the surface as per packet instructions, will be washed away into irregular lines when watered lightly – as per packet instructions.

THREAD'S UNIVERSAL PLUMB CRAZY LAW
   Threaded connections designed specifically to marry up with the standard BSP fittings already connected to the hose or attachments you have already purchased at great expense will be the last BSI standard bar two.

Things get worse under pressure

A SNAKE IN THE GRASS IS BETTER THAN A HOSE-PIPE IN THE HAND MAXIM

The new, flat, lightweight hose, beautifully braided in four colourways to blend with the garden and reinforced for extra strength and flexibility, will have no capacity at all to pass water. If, in the unlikely circumstance that it does manage to allow water to pass through, it will behave like a love-starved snake.

LAW OF REVERSE HUMOUR

The on/off trigger on a trigger-hose handle designed to cut off the flow of water as soon as you release the grip will immediately reverse the flow into:

1. Your midriff.

2. Someone else's midriff (they will be in their Sunday best).
3. The front seat of your car. This will only become apparent after parking the car early Monday morning and walking to the station.

COALS TO NEWCASTLE LAW
Oscillating sprays will spray the pond, the pool, the swimming pool and leave the lawn parched.

STRATEGEM ARTIFICES
All gadgets which turn your humble watering can or old hose into a quick and easy way to feed or water your garden will saturate you at some time or another. They will certainly be capable of drenching your neighbour's bedroom carpet.

LAW OF REELING
The hose which comes with its own special reel will become quite impossible to wind, either way, within a matter of days. If you can unwind and rewind it, the instructions tell you everything other than how to get the hose back in its holder without getting b. . . . . filthy.

ASA'S IGNORANCE OF WATERING-CAN BEHAVIOURAL PATTERNS
The art of using a watering can efficiently is to avoid water rushing from the can. It is impossible to hold the latest streamlined plastic cans at the angle shown by the nubile blonde in the illustration without producing a rush of water from the can.

THWART'S LAW OF APPLIED SOLUBLES
Anything dissolved in water and applied through a fine

rosed watering can or special dilutor, can and will clog the nozzle.

BITTER EXPERIENCE LAW
Expensive algae-killers block drains quicker than cheap varieties.

MOTHER HUBBARD'S LAW
The lack of any essential chemical means it is early closing day. Lime, fertilizers, insecticides and weed-killer eventually run out, despite all gardeners' belief in their everlasting qualities. You discover this halfway through a major project.

Thwart's law of applied solubles

8

Weather or Not

RAIN-MAKING RECIPES
1. Get the lawnmower out.
2. Water the garden.
3. Light the barbecue.
4. Throw a garden party.

DRY-UP SPELLS
1. Go abroad for a holiday.
2. Decorate the lounge.
3. Plant out seedlings.
4. Seed the lawn.

SUBJECT FOR DEBATE
Whoever discovers how to control the weather will have destroyed the last safe topic of conversation in or out of the garden.

PEEL'S LAW
Weather-resistant paint hasn't heard of the British summer.

MUM'S THE WORD
   As soon as you mention the weather: if it's good it goes away; if it's bad it happens.

GARDENING CATCH 22
   Enjoyment of the garden is prevented by weather. Fine weather means you're too busy working in the garden to enjoy it; when the weather worsens, it is too cold or wet to enjoy it.

THE BOOK OF TRUTH
   It doesn't explain why bad weather reports are more often spot on than good ones.

LOOK UP LAW
   If you wonder what's happened to the English summer, you may still be able to find it in the dictionary if you're quick.

HIAWATHA'S DEFINITION OF AN INDIAN SUMMER
   Apache clouds and bright spells.

LAW OF THE GARDEN ECONOMIST
   Saving for a rainy day ensures it will come.

PET PRINCIPLE
   A pessimist is someone whose face takes on the shape of the weather.

LAW OF BRITISH GARDENERS ARE LONG OVERDUE FOR SOME DECENT WEATHER
   Following a review of gardening policy in the British

Mum's the word

Isles, the Ministry of Agriculture, Fisheries and Food is to implement far-reaching, strategic weather measures with the aim of affecting a shift in the earth's axis. The result will be that Britain will occupy a new geographical location just ten degrees north of the equator. Manchester, for instance, will enjoy the climate of the Windward Isles. Southern Africa will therefore become the new South Pole and parts of China the new North Pole, while the polar icecaps will melt to create the two new vast temperate regions. Summer in Britain will be ten degrees warmer on average, with winter temperatures being maintained at a balmy 20°C. The Channel will be renamed 'The New Mediterranean'.

CLOUDED THOUGHTS
The use of a clouded crystal ball will in no way affect the

accuracy of clairvoyant predictions of the British weather.

WEATHER VANES
If every gardener has to have something to moan about in order to be happy, it may as well be the weather. Total misery is transformed to joy in a drought when he or she can explain that the catastrophic horticultural failure is not their fault but the weather's.

COUNT YOUR BLESSINGS
The finest thing about the future weather is that it only comes a day at a time.

THE BRITISH POSTULATE
The three constants in the garden are:

1. Too much sun.
2. Too much rain.
3. Not enough of either.

Corollary
Either whoever's up there just loves pressing the opposite weather key to the one a gardener needs, or He's a lousy typist.

MAKE YOUR BED AND LIE ON IT LAW
A keen gardener can be safely described as a person who sticks with troubles through rain or shine that he wouldn't have had in the first place had he or she not been a keen gardener.

BOGUS BELIEFS
A lot of what appears to be progress in the garden is due not to the gardener's skill but to weather, be it good or bad.

Bogus beliefs

9

Pets and Progeny

MESH MAXIM
The best-laid schemes of mice and gardeners gang aft a-gley, especially where cats and kids are concerned. It's one thing to install a cat-proof, child-proof seedling net. It's another thing to prove to the cats or children that they can't get through it.

KIDOLOGY
Children are always on their pest behaviour in the garden.

THE CAT TRAP
The only way for a cat hater to keep cats out of his garden is to get a moggy of his own.

BASIC LAW OF THE JUNIOR GARDENER
Children who have difficulty using a knife and fork have no trouble at all with gardening implements.

Corollary
People who give your small children miniature gardening tool sets, outdoor archery sets, footballs, etc. are bachelors, spinsters or sadists – or all three. They definitely don't have a garden of their own.

SEVEN RULES OF CHILD'S PLAY
1. Bulbs should be embedded with hammers.
2. Holes should be dug with chisels.
3. Nuts should be opened with hacksaws.
4. Lawns should be cut with daddy's razor.
5. Branches for dens should be loosened by swinging.
6. Gardens should be dug with the best silver.
7. Trays make good sledges.

THE DEAR, SWEET THINGS
The basic law propounded by midwives is that women love children. Any woman picking toys up from the garden will counter this.

Corollaries
1. Small children like helping daddy in the garden.
2. Children rarely tidy up their own mess in the garden; when they do, the compost heap is a favourite place to tidy into.
3. Your precious possessions, when dropped in the garden, vanish.

RALPH'S LAWS OF CREATION
1. Toddlers much prefer garden mud to modelling clay.
2. The more imaginative a child's creation, the more vital the space it occupies.
3. The psychological good done to a child by making mud pies is in direct proportion to the permanent psychological harm done to the gardener of the family when it is discovered that the recipe called for two pounds of John Innes No 1. Frogs make the

best filling.

Corollary
Don't eat home-made mud pies.

MON AMI LE CHAT **TRUISM**
The gardener who digs the garden thoroughly and regularly keeps the soil well-aired has a friend in the cat for life.

FATHER'S TRUISM
Children have nine lives. Their curiosity kills the cat.

Ralph's laws of creation (1)

BAMBOO LAWS
1. Stakes to support floppy plants are used by children to break the floppy plants they supported.

2. Bamboo canes make more realistic spears than those sold in the toy shop.

LAWS OF ATTRACTION AND REPULSION
1. Where dogs, cats and children are concerned, seedbeds and wet concrete have irresistible magnetic properties.

2. If you lay a path to protect the lawn and the flowerbeds you are simultaneously creating a force field which prevents children and animals from using it.

THE SUPREME TESTS OF PARENTHOOD
1. Letting your child and its friends help hoe the beds.

2. Giving your child its own little vegetable plot.

Corollary
A radish never tastes the same when you are told it was fed with cat manure.

LAW OF EXCRETIA DOGGIA
It is impossible to tell the size and type of a pet by the configuration on the lawn until you tread in it.

LAW OF THE FIRST ROW
The young mother who scolds her toddler for burying the dead fly in the seed bed, whilst covering up her toddler's tracks will discover that she has made a first-class job of digging up her husband's freshly sown seeds. This won't become apparent until ten days or so later.

Senor's truism

MRS GREEN'S HORTICULTURAL LAW
The mother who plants her five-year-old's half-dead Christmas tree out of sentiment will require a gang of professional tree-fellers about the time her child is twelve.

SENOR'S TRUISM
When a Mexican mobster peppers his peas, no cat ever digs them up.

Corollaries
1. Cats have a 50/50 chance of making it through the day.
2. Cats are immortal – whoever said they have only nine lives omitted a couple of zeros.

LAW OF THE PEACE ROSE
When your child arrives clutching a peace offering of mangled roses from the show bed, remember that rose is an anagram of 'Eros'.

FIREMAN'S TRUISM
The *Plain Truth Guide*, which holds the answer to most of life's burning questions, such as, 'Why doesn't God do something about insects and weeds?' doesn't explain why cats get stuck up trees.

You know how babies are made? Well, the birds and the bees do something similar

Birds and bees corollary

MRS MURPHY'S REPLY TO FIREMAN'S TRUISM
Because their tails point the wrong way, of course.

BLUEBELL'S LAMENT
Children enjoy watching flowers coming up – by the roots.

BIRDS AND BEES COROLLARY
The hardest part about telling young people the facts of fertilization is telling them something that they don't already know.

TOMATO LAWS (1)
Someone has to eat the products of the school's gardening lessons. A tomato is never the same when it has been brought home in a school satchel.

10

Weedology

LAW OF RESPITE
You always dreamed of a garden to relax in. Now you've got it, the time spent weeding it cancels out the time spent enjoying it.

PICK AND CHOOSE LAW
A basic law propounded by men is that they love all aspects of gardening. Any woman up to her neck in stinging nettles and deadly nightshade will counter this.

MRS MURPHY'S SPOKEN THOUGHTS
If weed-killer is so effective, why are there so many weeds?

HEROINE'S LAW
If our government is clever enough to control the world's largest narcotic rings, surely they can do something about eradicating my poppies?

JUSTIFIED SLOTH
Reasons against weeding the plot are always much more potent than those in favour.

CAPRICIOUS COMMENTS
Weeds are like rabbits – inordinately keen on breeding.

HILLARY'S OBSERVATION ON CONVOLVULUS
Climbers always help one another.

LAISSEZ-FAIRE FLUKE
Part of the layman's success in the garden is that he plants what he likes and lets the weeds and his contributions fight it out between them.

YARD RULE
Never let weeding interfere with gardening or your wife's sunbathing.

Old soldier's law

TARE'S REALITY
Weeds always move in to fill a gardening vacuum.

POMPOUS OVER-THE-FENCE OBSERVATION
Why do your weeds grow faster than mine?

OLD SOLDIER'S LAW
Old weeds never die, they simply fade away – until next spring.

ADAM'S RUMINATION
Weed-killer is lethal; spreading it is killing!

Corollary
Total weed-killer which, simply applied by spray, kills weeds in seconds, guarantees the arrival of unexpected guests. This will ensure that any trodden area will stay totally clear of any green living thing for up to three years. In the unlikely event that this does not happen, torrential rain will ensure that it will. Severe flooding of the paths will cause serious spillage on to your most prized beds.

SOD'S FIRST LAW OF THE GARDEN IN REPLY TO ADAM'S RUMINATION
If all else fails – plant concrete.

PROPAGATOR'S CHAPPAQUIDICK THEOREM (KENNEDY'S MISTAKE)
The sooner and more detailed your announcement that little Johnnie has watered the exhibition roses with weed-killer – the better.

Corollary
You can get away with anything as long as you tell someone else about it.

Law of the stately home visit

LAW OF THE SUCCESSFUL TARE AWAY
If it's thriving, it's probably a weed.

Corollaries
1. There is no such thing as a weed-free garden.
2. Useful or beautiful needs a lot of tending.
3. Anything useless will thrive.

CUCKOO SYNDROME
The wind always blows away the seed pack saying 'Beetroot' or 'Spinach'. So you end up transplanting five hundred or so dandelions.

FATAL ATTRACTION
The chance of the spray weed-killer drifting on to the roses is directly proportional to:
1. The worth of the blooms.
2. The shortness of time between that moment and the rose section of the Royal Horticultural Show.

Corollary
When spilled, there is no such thing as a 'little blood' or a 'little weed-killer'.

WEEDY WONDERS
1. One weed deserves another.
2. One weed leads to another.
3. Widow's weed.

LAW OF THE STATELY HOME VISIT
That cutting you swiped from Hever Castle turned out to be a self-seeding 7ft high, noxious weed. It is now invading the Lavatera area of the bog garden and killing off the goldfish (you later discovered they were Koi).

Corollary
The plant smuggled through Customs in your knickers belongs to the cannabis family.

PROVERBIAL TRUTH
A man of words and not of deeds is like a garden full of weeds.

WILD OATS MAXIM
Ill-gotten grains prosper.

JUST'S LAW
  Weeds are mean and fair at one and the same time – they grow abundantly for everyone.

BOARDROOM LAW
  A weed is a flower designed by a committee.

BLOW IT RULE
  If just one of your next-door neighbours cultivates waist-high weeds, you can bet your life that, when these go to seed, the wind will change course to blow every single one of those embryonic dandelions/couch grass/ground elder/rose-bay willow herbs on to your patch.

END OF THE ROAD
  The garden may be on the road to rack and ruin, but it won't get there with the present weed jam.

SILLY THOUGHTS
  Make your garden tick! Plant a dandelion clock.

The sleeping bulb fallacy

11

Blooming Truths

A FLORAL OFFERING
Say it with flowers – give her a cauliflower ear.

Corollary
If all else fails – call Interflora.

EVERLASTING FLOWERS
Words are the only things that last forever.

THE SLEEPING BULB FALLACY
There's no such thing as a dormant bulb or corm – they're all lurking underground ready to leap suicidally under the first fork prong or spade.

BLUSHING TRUTH
Silly flowers are tended by blooming idiots.

PINK'S LAW
No matter how long or hard you shop for bedding plants, after you've bought them from a nursery similar plants will be on sale on your local petrol station forecourt. They will be cheaper and sturdier.

Blushing truth

LAW OF ANTICIPATION
March winds and April showers bring forth May flowers – chickweed, dandelions, buttercups, etc.

STAY-IN-BED LAW
Peonies sulk for years if got up.

FIRST LAW OF THE BULBOUS
Bulbs prefer to be planted crown upwards – as if you can tell the difference!

Corollaries
1. No matter which way up you plant a bulb or corm, it'll probably turn out all right.
2. However deep and whichever way up you plant a snowdrop, it will always appear on the surface and sideways.

TRACK-STOPPING LAW
If herbaceous plants, valued neither for use or beauty,

growing wild or rank and regarded as cumbering ground or hindering growth of more valued plants, over-run the border, organize them into a committee – that should fix 'em.

LAW OF FLORICULTURE
Hardy annuals, such as sweet peas and cornflowers, which have a one-year lifespan, are, as the name suggests, completely impervious to everything – except pests, blight, animals, children, footballs, heavy rains, drought and high winds.

BORDER LINES
Border plants consist of tall plants, medium plants and dwarf plants. All will grow taller, or shorter than precise spacing has allowed for, e.g. those planted 3ft apart will be dwarf; those planted 1ft apart will grow to 3ft high and over.

Law of false hybrids

POOR LAW
The planting of any authentic 'foreign' garden will cripple any budget outside its country of origin.

LAW OF THE GOLDEN ROD
Perennials which come up year after year are best propagated by dividing and replanting the roots of established plants. The more essential it is to move a clump, the more vigorous the root system.

BIOLOGY APPLIED
Self-seeding flowers, pests and weeds are real enough, but the true enemy of the flower grower is Life.

RULE OF BLOOMIN' RELATIVES
Flowers are like people – people can choose their friends but are stuck with their relatives. People can make their own beds and, like flowers, have no choice but to lie on them.

FLOWERY OBSERVATIONS
1. The bee fertilizes the flower it plunders.
2. All flowers are gay.
3. Anything with exquisite charm or a rich fragrance will sting or scratch. If it does neither, it is poisonous.

FLORA'S COLOURBLIND THEOREM
The qualities which most attract a male to a female are the quality of her rosebuds – green fingers come after the marriage ceremony.

LAW OF FALSE HYBRIDS
Yellow snowdrops mean one of two things – you have a

dog or a visiting fox.

LAW OF SHOPPING BY POST
Post office strikes are timed to coincide with deliveries of late-ordered bulbs or bedding plants.

Corollary
Goods and services governed by the Mail Order Protection Scheme will exclude non-durable gardening products . . . as well as lucky pixies and gardening horoscopes.

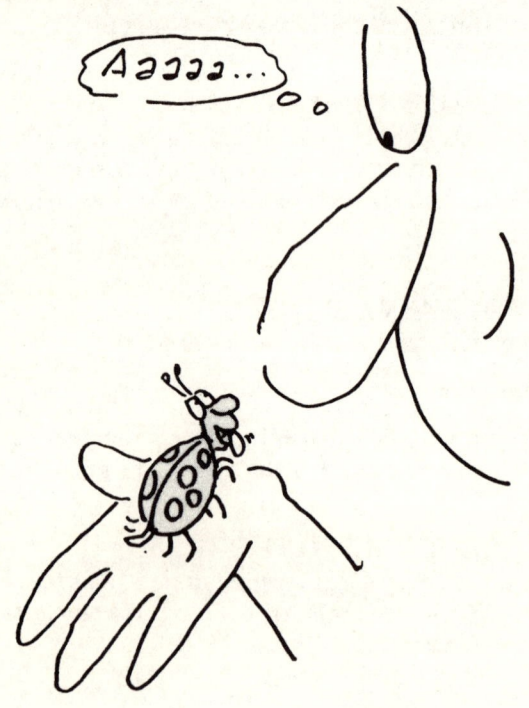

Greenfly's rueful observation

12

Bugs and Blights

ALTRUISM TRUISM
A garden is an area of land devoted to growing fruit, flowers and vegetables, which in turn are dedicated to insect rearing.

Corollaries
1. The earth is alive to the sound of mastication.
2. Healthy plants breed healthy bugs.

GREENFLY'S RUEFUL OBSERVATION
Why is it always my fault?

Corollaries
1. The prettier and more innocuous the insect appears to be, the further its influence will extend.
2. There's no point in worrying about infestation by aphids, blackfly and greenfly – if you have none, you soon will. That's a promise.
3. The worst thing about insects is insistency.

LAW OF CONTRADICTIONS
The function of the grower is to keep killing.

LAW OF THE VEGETABLE PATCH
A dose of insecticide which would wipe out a medium-size urban area will do no more than temporarily stun a cabbage white. You can fool all of the people some of the time, and some of the people all of the time, but you can't fool the caterpillars.

TOMATO LAWS (2)
The gardener who discovers he can grow tomatoes, grows tomatoes.

Corollaries
The survival of the aphid species is dependent on tomatoes.

POOR LAW
The cost of chemicals will cripple any enjoyment derived from a well-stocked, disease-free garden. A disease-ridden garden gives no one any pleasure.

SALAD DAYS
To find a slug – plant a lettuce.
The slug laughs all the way to the bank.

OBSERVATION ON SPONTANEOUS GENERATION
I swear blind I killed the little bleeders!

GARDENER'S BASIC LAW OF SOLUBLES AND SOLUTIONS
Any product offering general solutions to specific cultural problems creates specific problems requiring general solutions.

Corollaries
1. The chief cause of all problems in the garden is solutions.

2. It is only a problem when someone says it is.

BLIMP'S POSTULATE
Insects don't smoke or wash.

Corollary
During two world wars, soapy suds and nicotine made an excellent pesticide. Why doesn't it work now?

STOUT PRACTICES
If you spend time and energy rescuing a drone bee from the pond, the same bee will drown itself in the Guinness you left unquaffed in order to save that bee, rendering the brew undrinkable.

WEEVIL'S RULE
Get to the root of the matter.

CATERPILLAR'S LAW
Never underestimate a gardener's stupidity or the cook's knife!

COLESLAW INGREDIENTS
1. Root vegetables thinly shredded by pests.
2. Root vegetables carefully sliced by fork.

DI'S DIRE WARNING
In any calculation or task involving chemicals, any error which can creep in will do so, e.g. weed-killer on the lawn seeps into the pond and kills the fish.

Corollary
Any error in any calculation will result in the greatest possible damage, e.g. mother-in-law's pet cat eats dead fish and dies.

ADAMANT'S LAW OF FIRST FIND YOUR HILL
The power of the ant is not untrammelled. One can usually, with a little observation, discover at least two well-defined tracks leading to and from an ant's nest.

THE LAW OF LIFE AND DEATH
Never mind birds in the hand – get them out of the bush.

GARDENER'S STATEMENT
A toad is a gardener's best friend.

OLD CODGER'S REPLY TO THE ABOVE
Not when he pees on me and gives me warts he bain't.

REINCARNATION RECOMMENDATION
Gardeners have known for centuries what scientists have just discovered: the only living things capable of surviving a nuclear war are ants. The moral for Buddhists is clear – be naughty.

A WINNING ASIDE
In the fight between you, the world and the blight, back the blight.

PESTS IN THE MAKING
A female spider lays over two thousand eggs every time she's pregnant. It's just as well that she eats her mate, otherwise the world would be knee-deep in fornicating arachnids.

SALLY'S SIGH
When the insects take over the world, I bet they won't remember how the human race took them along on every picnic.

Sally's sigh

DEEP-END FALLACY
Gardeners often want to drown their sorrows; this is difficult as most insects can be taught to swim.

BILLY COTTON'S WAKEY-WAKEY LAW
In the garden, more deaths occur in bed than out. The obvious answer is to force everything out of bed.

CHARITY'S BELIEF
Everyone should have a cause. Build a pond and befriend a mosquito. When you starve with a mosquito the mosquito starves last.

UNSOLVED CRIMES
The difficulty of finding or identifying any given parasite is directly proportional to the importance of the consequences of failing to identify it.

RALPH'S LAW OF GARDENING
Do unto unsects before they do it to you.

LAW OF KILLING GENEROSITY
Don't look a gift horse in the mouth, but if it comes from a garden centre, do check for Trojan aphids somewhere in its anatomy.

SWINGS AND ROUNDABOUTS THEORY
The total amount of devastation in any garden remains constant. Therefore, any diminution in one direction (e.g. cremate infected crops, spray with flowers of sulphur, early application of sulphate of iron, ad nauseam) is met and accompanied by an increase in another (e.g. bugs).

ATHEISTIC INSECTS AXIOM
No insect believes in God. Does God believe in insects?

APHIDS LAW OF FALL-OUT
Pound for pound, virus-carrying greenflies are more lethal than the nuclear bomb.

FAITH'S LAW OF CYBERNETIC ENTOMOLOGY
Butterflies come and go, but caterpillars chew on forever.

PEST LAW
The sum of infestation in the garden is constant: the population is growing.

LAW OF NATURE
Anything in the garden goes.

FAITH'S LAW OF AUTHORSHIP
It's easier to knock up a book on gardening and to get rid of writer's block when writing it than getting rid of aphids on the roses.

PEACE AND QUIET WARNING (VERA'S ADVICE)
When all is quiet on the Gardening Front – something's up. When the dawn chorus stops, it signals breakfast has begun.

Corollaries
1. 'There'll be fat birds over, the white cliffs of Dover – tomorrow, cultivate and see.'
2. Everything in the garden is edible.
3. Whilst humans propose radical moralities, the birds and the bees can get on with the seven deadly sins.

NEW GARDENER'S MAXIM
Quality is the keystone of a good garden. The design, material and plant selection of your average slug endorses this.

Corollaries
1. There's no period of time whatever between dormant and shoot in slug-land.
2. The difference between quick and dead is going to the door to assure the gentleman you don't want your drive Tarmacked.
3. Any thistle can progress between germination and six foot tall without ever passing through nibbled.

13

Undercover Revelations

LAW OF POSSIBILITIES
Those that are fortunate enough to own a greenhouse are unlimited in their potential for horticultural disasters.

LAW OF THE HOTHOUSE
Under the most vigorously controlled conditions – temperature, humidity, ventilation, cultural routine, hygiene and other variables – bugs, beetles, caterpillars, slugs and flies will do as they damn well please.
If the bugs don't get them, grey mould, chlorosis, fungal and virus disease will.

TEMPERATURE LAWS
1. The slow-burning furnace in the greenhouse slows down to extinction on the coldest night of the year.
2. The particular virtue of electricity in the greenhouse is that it need only be used when the temperature requires it. When temperature levels are vitally important – during a very cold snap – the nation's gardeners' electricity demands will exceed the capacity of the National Grid.
3. A kaput fuse has the same capacity as the National Grid to cause havoc in the greenhouse.

I thought we might buy a greenhouse...

4. Labour-saving oil heaters need refilling daily – somebody has to fetch the fuel.

5. In summer, the greenhouse lights refuse to open – in winter they refuse to close.

NEW YEAR'S RESOLUTION OBSERVATIONS

During the short, almost dismal, days of the New Year, there is no more welcome sight than the brilliant colours of indoor primulas and cinerarias – if you had remembered to sow them.

Corollary
To enjoy anything in the greenhouse you must start the year before.

WET NURSE COUNSEL
If great care is taken in the greenhouse or hotbed to ensure seedlings don't dry out, some helpful person will overwater them, killing them. You will be accused of not watering soon and often enough.

OUT OF SIGHT, OUT OF MIND
Seeds carefully sown, given gentle heat and covered with paper, polythene and glass to encourage germination, will be remembered weeks late when they have developed into seedlings and died through chlorophyll starvation.

Corollary
Seeds thrown accidentally on a waste patch of ground in the depths of winter and left untended will develop into prize blooms.

PARANOIA SYNDROME
Tendency to sleep (or hide) in the greenhouse guarding prize produce from things that go chomp in the night.

PUNK LAW
If your new pot plant sweats and breaks out in pustules, check that you haven't brought home the shop assistant by mistake.

NURSERYMAN'S ANSWER TO PUNK LAW
It was six foot until I gave it a haircut. Now I've discovered it's five foot nothing. My punk grandson had taken root.

COLONEL'S COMMENT ON HARDENING OF HIS DAPHNE

Being a teeny-weeny bit on the cold side, it is a bit slower than most, but when it does its thing, it is quite, quite beautiful.

Corollary

1. The retired military man who talks about pricking out his Daphnes in his hotbed may have other nasty habits too.

2. Don't air your auriculas in public.

Rubber plant's inflation truism

CONSERVATORY MAXIMS
1. Extend your garden indoors: buy welly boots for all the family.
2. The conservatory is a room for all seasons: hot when it's hot, cold when it's not.

RUBBER PLANT'S INFLATION TRUISM
1. Nurseries and garden centres specialize in offering bigger and better . . . prices.
2. Procreation always repeats itself – every time the price goes up and up and up.

14

Produce Principles

POSTMAN PAT'S POSTULATE
Never stamp on an envelope-size plot.

USEFUL HINTS FOR THE OWNER OF A POCKET GARDEN
If you sow seeds between rows of established crops to make full use of the limited ground available, Sod's Laws of the Garden One and Two apply.

SOD'S LAW OF THE GARDEN (1)
Seeds sown too close never mature.

SOD'S LAW OF THE GARDEN (2)
If by chance they do mature, they will choke each other to death.

Corollary
If cramped surroundings don't get them, carbon-monoxide will.

ONION SET QUESTION
Why didn't they put a label on it saying 'crocus', then?

THE HOME PRODUCER'S LAMENT
Everything matures at the same time. Just as it does, the

Housekeeper's homily

abundance of summer will pour into the stores, bringing sharp price cuts. Not only does this coincide with everything in your garden crying out to be picked, shelled, washed, blanched and packed for the freezer instantly, the collapse in prices makes your efforts to save money downright laughable. In any event, all your friends will leave crumpled carrier bags full of their excess runner beans, peas, strawberries, etc. on your front doorstep – they won't stop to ring the bell in case you say, 'No thank you'. In every case, the freezer will still be full of this year's glut when you're ready to store next year's crop.

Corollary
You get the most of what you want the least.

LAW OF PLENTY
The number of any given relatives, friends, business colleagues and acquaintances a gardener may have at any given time varies in direct proportion to the season, i.e. whether the raspberries and strawberries are ripe.

Corollaries
1. The number increases or decreases with the type of gardener – the one who picks the fruit for you and the one who says, 'Help yourself'.
2. Nothing from the country garden is given away, except for a very good reason.

THE LAW OF HOMEGROWN IS BEST
A late second-cropping British strawberry, however tasteless, beats a dozen imported early Californians.

PEAS' QUANDARY
Who Feltham First?

HOUSEKEEPER'S HOMILY
People who believe a carrot screams when pulled make you feel you know each vegetable personally.

AN ASSLICKER'S STOCK ADVICE
If you don't grow your own fruit and veg., get wise! Praise and admire the produce of those who do.

THREE LAWS OF THE VISITING GARDENER OR HEINZ SITE
In gardening a mistake presented with conviction is a creation. If a visiting gardener says the garden is interesting, it's a failure. Behind every successful haricot bean is an astonished in-law.

STRINGFELLOW'S AXIOM
Runner beans are highly strung.

Corollaries
1. Give a runner bean and a lie a twenty-four hour start and you'll never overtake either.
2. Any runner bean can pass from being too young to too old without ever passing through 'edible'.

LAW OF GLUT
The trouble with overspill is that you find yourself being nice to neighbours you never liked.

Corollary
When the radish season is at its height, a neighbour in need is a friend indeed.

MS MUESLI'S FIBRE CLAIM
When I go on a vegetable diet, the first thing I lose is my appetite . . . followed by my temper.

Corollary
Before the advent of Channel 4, no one knew what a vegetable thought.

SPUD'S LAWS
1. The fork tines always find the best potatoes.
2. A seed-potato planted with meticulous care on a well rotted compost base, in precisely spaced drills, and earthed up as growth develops, will never better the quality of the vast quantities of fungus-free potatoes produced by the potato parings chucked on the rubbish heap.
3. However thoroughly you lift the haulms and clear the ground, one tuber will remain. This will produce

luxuriant foliage swamping next year's seed bed and robbing the seedlings of vital nutrients.

LOCAL'S WARNING
Duck eggs.
Heavy plant crossing (archaic).

IT'S A PLOT
It is said that what makes root vegetables and politicians crooked is following the line of least resistance. If then, politicians are, say like potatoes (the best ones are underground), all conversations with a carrot should be held strictly in private.

ETHNIC MINORITY LAW
A vegetable cult means that not enough people eat it to make a majority.

15

Machination Ruminations

LAW OF ASSEMBLY
Anything easily dismantled is mantled with disconcerting difficulty.

TECHNOLOGY MAXIM
Gardening is the irresistible march of the machine versus the unstoppable advance of nature.

MURPHY'S CONSTANT
The perceived usefulness of a powered gardening tool or mechanical gardening apparatus is inversely proportional to its actual claimed usefulness once bought and paid for.

Corollary
Manufacturer's performance specifications should be multiplied by a factor of 0·5. Sales people's claims for performance by a factor of 0·25.

MURPHY'S MECHANICAL LAWS OF GARDENING
1. Other people's tools work only in other people's gardens.
2. Fancy gizmos don't work.
3. If nobody uses it, there's a reason.
   (Apologies to *Murphy's Law*.)

Murphy's mechanical laws of gardening (2)

TUNGSTEN TIP
A sharp tongue is the only edged tool that stays sharper with use.

IRIS'S LITERARY TRUISMS
Any installation, operating instruction and guarantee delivered with any machine will be promptly discarded by the wife. If all else fails, empty the trash can for instructions. In the unlikely event that the instructions are found, the following laws apply:

1. The instructions will be in Chinese. If you are

Chinese, they will be written in English.
2. If you can understand the instructions, any part requiring adjustment will be in the most inaccessible position.
3. A smattering of Chinese, Latin or Anglo-Saxon English helps when applying brute force and ignorance.

SPARE FACTS

Every good gardener has a reserve of odd handles. No handle fits any tool. If a handle by chance fits, the wood will be rotten. However, this will not be apparent until the tool is in use.

Corollaries
1. Buckets with holes have handles.
2. Handles have no buckets.
3. Sieves have no sides.

RED RAG LAW

If, in a gardening practice or situation, a safety factor is set through in-service experience at an ultimate value, an ingenious gardener will promptly calculate a method of exceeding the said ultimate value.

OLD WIVES' TALE

It's quicker to dig the plot with a knife and fork than to clean and disembowel the rotovator after each use.

ADAM'S COGENT COMMENTS

1. You are not a gardener until you've pierced your foot with a fork.
2. If you pierce too many feet with a fork, you're no gardener.

3. A fool and his foot are soon parted.

MOTOR AXIOM
If your new mower features a powerful 23 cc engine and if it has electronic ignition and if it has an any angle carburettor, the nylon pull-start will snap. If the nylon pull-start doesn't snap, you will be out of fuel or oil or both. Should you add oil to the fuel, you will discover that the engine is not a two-stroke and will not function with additives.

THE PRINCIPLE OF SECOND THOUGHTS
People think agricultural machines should work – pity machines can't think!

JOHNSON'S FIRST LAW
When any mechanical contrivance fails, it will do so at the most inconvenient time possible.

TOOLS TRUISM
Design a garden tool that even a fool can use and only a fool will want to use it.

WATSON'S LAW
The reliability of a chain-saw is inversely proportional to the number and significance of people looking at it.

OPERATIONAL LAW
Any machine which promises dramatic improvements in garden maintenance needs someone to operate and maintain it.

Corollaries
1. Any machine is only as efficient as its operator.
2. Any new machine hailed as 'amazing', 'labour-saving' and a 'boon to busy gardeners' will become the centre

of a design fault scandal the minute it becomes your most indispensable possession.

MURPHY'S COROLLARY TO THE OPERATIONAL LAW
If it jams – force it. If it breaks, it needed replacing anyway.

SORE'S LAW
If the saw isn't heavy and cumbersome, the handle will give you blisters. If the handle doesn't give you sores and blisters, your hand will drop off at the wrist.

CABLE AXIOM
Any portable, indispensable powered machine with quick-change heads which deals with a multitude of jobs in and around the house and garden will be an inch short of cable wherever you need to use it.

THE LAW OF SAWING IS BELIEVING
The super saw that cuts through marble, bricks, metal, tiles and rubber with ease, won't cut beansticks.

HILL'S LAW
Hiding all the spades will not stop the moles digging.

BITS AND PIECES MAXIM
The only pieces missing when you finally locate the tool are the blades, multi-position locking nuts, bits, etc. The tool is useless without them.

TOUCH-ME-NOT MAXIM
A spade gives a wise man something to think about and

a foolish woman something useful to dig with.

Corollary
Anybody who slings mud loses ground.

TRUNDLE'S TRUISM
When eliminating all unnecessary equipment while loading the barrow to take to the far end of the plot, the first thing you decide to leave in the shed will be the first thing you need.

Corollaries
1. When unloading a wheelbarrow, if you put away the tool you are sure you have dispensed with, you will need it the moment you reach the opposite end of the garden.
2. The bottom of the barrow will fall out only if it contains manure or cement.
3. Most people have a wheelbarrow with a non-working wheel.

EVE'S COMMENTS ON TOOLS
1. Hands came before tools and knives and forks.
2. A man might insist there is a right tool for the job, a place for everything and everything in its place: a woman puts it into practice.

ADAM'S CAUTION
Never tread on a rake.

HANDS-UP HOMILY
Whoever operates the chain-saw makes the rules.

CHILD'S PLAY CONUNDRUM

Parts that positively cannot be assembled in the wrong order will be. For example, interchangeable parts aren't; the leaf machine will blow, not suck; the replacement leaf bag won't fit.

Adam's caution

16

Trees and Shrubbery

CELSIUS CURSE
Anything that survives the coldest and wettest summer since records began will perish during the mildest winter on record.

PERMAFROST PRINCIPLE
All delivery promises must be multiplied by a factor of east wind plus hard frost. In other words, all new shrubs, bulbs and trees will arrive during a six-week period of hard ground frost. The bushes must be left heeled-in until the weather improves: it is impossible to break the soil surface to heel them in.

FIRST LAW OF ARBORICULTURE
The magnificent mature tree you spotted in the National Trust garden and a similar sapling bought later at your local nursery at great expense take a hundred years to mature. No one told you this. Even if you did live to see it, the full-grown tree wouldn't look the same in your garden.

PEKE'S PERDITION
Plant four trees and your neighbour's dog won't have a

First law of arboriculture

leg to stand on.

COBBER'S PLEA
Help to green-up Australia – plant an acorn upside down.

AU SOLEIL
The carefully selected, ideal situation chosen for the specimen, shade-loving shrub in November will get the full force of the sun all summer.

RIGHT ANGLE
Are box hedges square or the square root of all evil?

BLOOMER'S OBSERVATION
If everything seems to be coming up roses, it probably is.

Corollary
Not every gardener can distinguish one young shrub (or grub, for that matter) from another.

ROOTLESSNESS TRUISM
A tree that has one end has another. This applies except when you transplant it. Then it has no visible roots.

ILL WIND FALLACY
Gales will uproot only your favourite shrubs.

Corollary
If you want to get rid of an unfavourite shrub, no matter how deep you dig, the roots will not give way.

PIPPIN'S LAW
The worm in the crab apple doesn't know any better.

LEAF LAW
People with swimming pools shouldn't plant trees.

Corollary
People in glasshouses shouldn't throw stones.

ACID TESTINESS
The tree you selected with the utmost care from the mail order catalogue is precisely the one that doesn't do well in your acid soil. You will discover this only after the tree has died and the company refuses to refund your money.

PINE'S PROTEST
Christ didn't tell us to kill trees for Christmas.

EVERGREEN'S TRUISM
There's no such thing as a cheap tree or shrub.

LAW OF PLANTERS CAN'T BE CHOOSERS
A gardener who is hunting for shrubs or trees looks first

Evergreen's truism

at the specimens suitable for his land, then at the substitutes on his list, and finally buys the one he can afford.

LAWS OF TREE PLANTING
1. Turn any turf to plant a specimen tree and you'll hit solid concrete. If, however, you find an area where you can dig a hole large and deep enough to allow the roots to spread, the tree will:
   a. Obscure the garden from every window.
   b. Obliterate all light to the house in two years.
   c. Activate a dormant spring.
2. The only item the nursery forgot to supply is the free stake with every tree. Not only did they forget to send it, ninety-nine per cent of the time they haven't even made it. If you ask for it, there is no demand; if you wait for it, the tree will snap in the first mild gust of wind.

3. If a supporting stake is supplied it will not be found until the roots are fully covered and each spadeful of soil returned, trodden down firmly and the turf replaced. The stake will severely damage the feeding roots of the tree. If the stake cannot be driven in easily, it will be discovered that the hole is surrounded by solid concrete left by the contractors.
4. Any tree left unstaked will eventually snap and die.

SCRUMP'S LAW
Broken glass bottles and jars cemented into six-foot walls means two of three things:
1. The owner has something to hide.
2. He doesn't like children.
3. There are apples behind that there wall!

LAW OF AMBITION
Inside every rose bush is a climber trying to get out.

AMATEUR'S RULES
If the root's too long, bend it.
If it won't bend, force it.
If it breaks, the tree would have died anyway.
In all cases it is the nurseryman's fault.
Nobody ever thinks of digging a larger hole – they buy a smaller tree with the refund.

EVE'S OFFER
The days of lofty fruit trees, occupying valuable room and endangering life and limb when picking, are past. The sensible modern technique involves trees whose height never exceeds twelve feet.
The great advantage is that the trees can be pruned and scrumped without stretching.

17

Garden Decor

CREATIVE THOUGHT
Landscaping is a symptom of decay.

LAW OF SKIMMING
The person who cleans the swimming pool rarely has time to swim in it.

GNOMIC PONDERING
The astonishing anthropomorphic success of garden gnomes is based on the simple British proposition that dirty old men are lovable if they wear red hats.

LAW OF SUPPLY AND DEMAND
Well-stocked ponds attract people – people attract mosquitoes – mosquitoes are stocked with blood – fish eat mosquitoes.

Corollary
The local density of stinging and biting insects is inversely proportional to the amount of remaining repellent in the canister.

POT LUCK
The finely proportioned pot you bought at the

ridiculously expensive antique shop and which you thought was the exact type, shape, colour and size for your recently completed colonnade will:

1. Clash: the colour stands out like a new sore thumb.

2. If the colour doesn't clash, it will be either too high or too wide.

3. Everything else in the garden will need changing to match.

DROP-IN DISCOVERY
The most direct way from the garage to the back door is via the new pond: this will not become apparent until after dark.

LINER'S LAW
A pool liner is never long enough.

Corollary
If a liner is long enough one way it won't reach the other.

LAW OF ARCHITECTURE
By the time you've saved for that specimen statue you spotted three years ago at the repro-shop to stand midst the rhodies and azaleas:

1. Those of suitable size will be priced out of your pocket despite the sensational drop in inflation.
2. The shrubs will need replacing and you can't afford both.

THE CRACKED PLATE SYNDROME
1. Everything in the garden falls apart sooner or later.
2. Bindweed keeps sheds together indefinitely.

ANOTHER COUPLE OF INCHES LAW
Any fool who thinks a pool is simply a hole in the ground, filled with water, has never tried to make water level with the surrounding ground.

Corollary
No pool looks aslant until it has been filled with water.

DESIGNER BOOBS
However professional the garden plan or drawing, the

most vital part stands the greatest chance of being omitted. For example, the Yorkstone will be placed and the terraces cemented before the drains and the electricity for that essential lighting are laid.

DISASTER THOUGHTS

Major changes in construction will always be requested when a landscaped garden is almost complete, e.g. 'I don't like the swimming-pool there'.

MA'S LAW OF ALL PROBLEMS ARE REPRODUCIBLE

In the extremely unlikely event that all major underground work is complete prior to the laying and cementing of the new, expensive patio surface, the gas, electric or water board will suspect a leak. After no less than ten tonnes of slab and hardcore has been removed, it will be discovered they are digging at the wrong address. However carefully the hardcore and stones are relaid, an enormous pile of rubble and a couple of slabs will remain excess to requirements. In a matter of weeks, severe frost will cause a mains fracture. It will be precisely where they dug before. This time you will be left with twice the rubble and several more stones excess to requirements.

Corollary
Those large slabs and the rubble you couldn't wait to get rid of which today were taken by a kind friend to the tip are exactly what you need this afternoon after oil soundings have been conducted in the area. Neither the council nor the oil company will be responsible for the cavity or for replacing the material or making good the damage.

LAW OF THE PYROMANIAC

Why use firelighters to light charcoal when petrol will do?

Law of the pyromaniac

KITE'S FUNDAMENTALS RELATING TO THE PRESERVATION OF FENCES

1. a. If the paint or preservative is harmless to plants, it will kill the goldfish.

   b. If it is clean, quick and simple to use, the large-sized brush recommended won't fit the pot.

   c. If the brush fits the pot and the paint doesn't write off the goldfish, the plants will probably die anyway.

2. a. If it is claimed the colour lasts a lifetime, it will outlast the life of the fence or seat.

    b. The newly treated fence, guaranteed to last a lifetime and harmless to all living creatures, will collapse under the weight of healthy bee-laden honeysuckle, clobbering the family tortoise in the process.

3. All paints that go a lot further, do. Every available shelf space in the house and garage will be crammed with almost empty pots. No pot will contain sufficient paint to complete any job. If, by remarkable coincidence, one does contain enough for a touch-up job, the colour will bear no resemblance whatsoever to its original colour. The entire fence will have to be repainted.

SPARE TIME (OR MORE SILLY THOUGHTS)
My sundial is half an hour fast – is this a record?

JAWS 3 POOLSIDE THOUGHT
Just as you thought it was safe to put your hand into the filter . . .

LAW OF THE B.B.Q.
All the merchandise guaranteed against defects in materials and workmanship does not take into account the idiot or the British weather.

Corollaries
1. The grill with two positions incinerates in both.
2. Motorized spits pack up on the one sunny weekend of the summer.

NEWTON'S SLIDE RULE
Heavy objects and jagged rockery stones gravitate towards ponds with plastic liners. They will wait until

the pond is fully planted, stocked, naturalized and thriving before making holes.

CEMENTING FRIENDSHIPS

However much cement you mix, it is either never quite enough or much too much. Nothing can be done with the excess, except to tip it into the pond. Cement kills goldfish – no one told you to wait six months before stocking the pool with fish.

Cementing friendships

18

Pot Hunting

SIX REQUIREMENTS FOR WINNING AT THE LOCAL FLOWER AND VEGETABLE JAMBOREE
1. A few quid – around ten – does it.
2. A teenage wife – the blonder the better and 38D or over.
3. A teenage husband – if the judges are female.
4. Membership of either the Police Federation, the Freemasons, or the local church.
5. A glib tongue.
6. Absolutely no knowledge of Latin.

Exceptions to the above rules

If at least one relative is titled, or a chief constable, a win can be taken for granted in one or all classes. In every case, absolutely no knowledge of gardening is required.

MOTHER-IN-LAW'S TONGUE TRUISM
If you manage to grow fruit and vegetables to exhibition criteria, they'll never in a month of Sundays equal those of your in-laws' standards.

GARDENER'S PRAYER FOR HARVEST FESTIVAL
O Lord, grant that I may grow a marrow so big that I may never again have to lie about it.

LAW OF THE CHRYSANTHEMUM
The most brilliant, the most perfect, the most magnificent bloom will usually lose.

Corollary
No exhibition bloom is totally worthless: it can always be used by other competitors as a disastrous example.

LAW OF THE LOSS LEADER
Any bloom or vegetable grown successfully a hundred times before, to universal acclaim, will fail the minute you are persuaded to enter the county show.

DUTCH COURAGE, OR THE LAW OF THAT'S SHALLOT
Having the bottle to tell father you mistook his stored tulip bulbs for onions.

JUDGE CARTER'S THREE WINNING RULES
1. When it comes to corruption, nothing succeeds like money.
2. Judges believe anything if it is passed on a piece of paper or whispered in their ear.
3. Get drunk with top people.

LAWS OF THE N.C.S.
Having transported the blooms safely to the show, staged them and positioned them where they can't be knocked over, you will discover the schedule was worded so badly and obscurely that your entry doesn't qualify.

Judge Carter's winning rule (2)

GOURD LAWS
1. To make a real enemy – grow a larger pumpkin.
2. Trust everybody, but chain your pumpkin to your leg at the show.

BASIC RULES FOR WOULD-BE COMPETITION WINNERS
1. Smile – it makes the other competitors wonder what

you have up your sleeve.
2. Wear a green carnation in your buttonhole.
3. Shake as many hands as possible – yell 'Sarah', 'Andy' and 'Frosty' (or any other media names you can think of).
4. Avoid making speeches.
5. If you have bribed the judges or organizers, donate your prize to the raffle.
6. Above all, remain amazed that *you* have won.

EVERYONE A COCONUT TRUISM
Enter any competition – gardening or otherwise – and you'll receive junk mail for life.

LOSER'S FIRST RULE
Losing at the W.I. Fruit and Vegetable Show is not a matter of life and death – it's much more important than that.

RUEFUL COMMENTS BY A MAD MAN
If you tell the truth once about how you came to grow the pumpkin featured in *The Guiness Book of Records*, no one will ever believe what you say again, however much you lie.

ROSE'S REVELATION
The convincing winner is the one who can keep his hands in his pockets while describing the size of the bloom he didn't bring.

VICAR'S ADDRESS
. . . and the beautiful flowers and vegetables of the show

will be distributed to those who are sick after I have finished...

BOLT'S LAWS OF DONATION
1. All prize vegetables are tough and flavourless.
2. Anything inedible but which looks good is donated to the old folk's home.

DEFINITION OF INCREDIBILITY
Look on competitor's face when he knows you can't have won.

LAW OF MORTIFICATION
Tendency to reproach yourself for not being able to accept your competitor's defeat.

HOW TO SPOT A GUILTY FOOL
Tendency to hurl himself on to the compost heap when, after carefully swapping his pumpkin at the Church Show for another's – his wins!

OPTIMIST'S LAW
Bliss is the interval between the last payment on the greenhouse and the first repair bill.
If the repair bill doesn't get you, the heating bill will. If neither apply, every other law of indoor culture will.

MRS PLATO'S OBSERVATIONS
When Murphy dies, he hopes to discover the riddle of the Perfumed Garden.
When Mrs Murphy dies, she hopes to visit the Garden of Eden and give the tree its flipping apple back!